marie claire

pasta

acknowledgements

Firstly, I would like to thank Anne Wilson and Catie Ziller for the opportunity to realise a long-term dream and for their continued encouragement and support. Jane Price, my wonderful editor, for sorting out my word salad. Anna Waddington, the most organised gentle woman, who did such a fabulous job co-ordinating this series. The talented Marylouise Brammer for her beautiful design. Lulu, Kathy, Jane and Rebecca for lending their tasting buds and being such knowledgeable sisters in the kitchen. Special thanks to Ben Dearnley, my photographer, and Kristen Anderson, my stylist, whose combined talents speak for themselves in this book. To Michaela Le Compte, who helped me test recipes and did such a magnificent job preparing the food for photography. And finally a few extra special thank yous... To my friend and mentor, the lady princess Donna Hay, who taught me that anything is possible if you focus, work hard and maintain your sense of humour. To my mum, Matt, Tracey, Paulie, Narelle, Rhearn and Nathan, whose unconditional love allows me to constantly test my boundaries. To Dundee, who always has time to offer the most sensible heartfelt advice. To Daz, Annie, Mel, Jude, Nicci, Mel, Michael, Shem and Gabe for being true friends and ever-willing guinea pigs and sounding boards. And, finally, to my dearest most honoured and cherished friend Penel, this is for you. Cheers.

The publisher wishes to thank the following for their generosity in supplying props for the book: Bison Homewares; Orrefors Kosta Boda; Inne Transform; Myer Grace Bros; Funkis Swedish Forms; Plane Tree Farm; White; The Bay Tree; Country Road Australia; Shack; Wheel & Barrow; Culti; Mud Australia.

Front cover: crunchy primavera spaghetti, page 72.

marie claire

pasta

jody vassallo

MURDOCH BOOKS®

Sydney • London • Vancouver • New York

contents

Our pasta dishes are a meal in themselves, but if you want to dress them up with some simple salad ideas, try...

teardrop tomatoes, lightly tossed in sea salt and sprinkled with oregano

blanched asparagus with roasted hazelnuts and a drizzle of balsamic

baby cos, prosciutto and parmesan shavings with herb mayonnaise

thin-sliced orange and watercress in a dressing of honey, oil and mustard

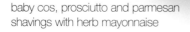

preserved lemon and fresh flat-leaf
parsley with feta cheese

rocket leaves with vine-ripened
tomatoes and shaved pecorino

avocado, toasted pine nuts, snow
pea sprouts and a little balsamic

young witlof (chicory) leaves with
shards of creamy blue cheese

Team up our pasta dishes with the following breads...

chunks of white bread, toasted and smothered with pesto and parmesan

lavash bread brushed with oil, honey and balsamic and baked until crisp

french baguette topped with sun-dried capsicum and rocket leaves

hunks of ciabatta dipped in rosemary-infused olive oil.

crunchy toasted bread with fresh
ricotta cheese and roasted garlic

thickly sliced turkish pide with olive
tapenade and sprigs of thyme

puff pastry sprinkled with parmesan
and caraway seeds, rolled and baked

wood-fired bread dipped in extra
virgin olive oil, topped with parmesan

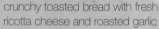

Take care not to overcook fresh
tuna. It should be served
medium rare and succulent.

pepper tuna with chervil and capers

500 g (1 lb) farfalle
500 g (1 lb) tuna steaks
6 cloves garlic, crushed
cracked black pepper
1 tablespoon oil
4 ripe roma tomatoes, finely chopped
3 tablespoons capers
extra virgin olive oil
3 tablespoons lime juice
2 tablespoons chopped fresh chervil

Cook the pasta in a large pan of rapidly
boiling water until al dente. Drain and
return to the pan.

Coat the tuna on both sides with the
crushed garlic, then toss in the cracked
black pepper.

Heat the oil in a large heavy-based
frying or chargrill pan and cook the tuna
over high heat until medium rare.
Remove from the pan and leave for
5 minutes before cutting into thin slices.
Add the tuna (with any juices) to the
pasta. Add the tomato, capers, oil, lime
juice and chervil. Toss together and
serve immediately.

Serves 6

Capelli d'angelo is Italian for 'angel hair'. These thin noodles are as fine as the hair of angels.

balsamic capsicum on angel hair

Cook the pasta in a large pan of rapidly boiling water until al dente, then drain. Cut the capsicums into large flat pieces and place under a hot grill until the skins blister and blacken. Leave to cool in a plastic bag, then peel away the skin and cut the flesh into thin strips. Combine the capsicum, garlic, orange juice and balsamic vinegar. Drizzle over the pasta. Serve topped with crumbled goats cheese, basil and a sprinkling of cracked black pepper.

Serves 4

300 g (10 oz) angel hair pasta
2 red capsicums (peppers)
2 yellow capsicums (peppers)
2 green capsicums (peppers)
4 cloves garlic, crushed
2 tablespoons orange juice
80 ml (2 3/4 fl oz) balsamic vinegar
100 g (3 1/2 oz) goats cheese
1/2 cup fresh basil leaves
cracked black pepper, for serving

Pastitsio is a Greek pasta dish. We've used beef mince but the recipe is equally good with lamb.

pastitsio

2 tablespoons oil
4 cloves garlic, crushed
2 onions, chopped
1 kg (2 lb) beef mince (ground beef)
1 kg (2 lb) canned peeled tomatoes, chopped
250 ml (8 fl oz) dry red wine
250 ml (8 fl oz) beef stock
1 bay leaf
1 teaspoon dried mixed herbs
350 g (11 oz) ziti
3 eggs, lightly beaten
500 g (1 lb) greek-style yoghurt
200 g (6 1/2 oz) kefalotyri cheese, grated
1/2 teaspoon ground nutmeg
1/2 cup grated cheddar cheese

Heat the oil in a large heavy-based pan, and cook the garlic and onion over medium heat for 5 minutes, or until the onion is soft. Add the mince and cook over high heat until browned, then drain off any excess fat. Add the tomato, wine, stock, bay leaf and herbs and bring to the boil. Reduce the heat and simmer for 40 minutes. Season well. Meanwhile, cook the pasta in a large pan of rapidly boiling water until al dente. Drain well and spread in the base of a large ovenproof dish. Pour in half the egg and top with the sauce. Combine the yoghurt, remaining egg, kefalotyri and nutmeg and pour over the top. Sprinkle with the cheddar and bake for 40 minutes, or until golden brown. Leave to stand for 10 minutes before serving.

Serves 6–8

For seafood lovers, this is a wonderful 'special occasion' pasta dish that's hard to beat.

layered seafood pasta salad

Cook the scallops in simmering water for 3 minutes, or until white and tender. Drain and place in a bowl with the yabbies, prawns and mussels. Drizzle with lime juice and olive oil and sprinkle generously with cracked black pepper. Toss to coat and refrigerate while you cook the pasta and make the dressing. Cook the pasta in a large pan of rapidly boiling water until al dente, then drain. To make the dressing, place all the ingredients in a food processor and mix well. Add half the dressing to the pasta and toss together. Arrange the rocket on a large chilled platter. Top with the pasta and then the seafood. Drizzle with the remaining dressing and serve with lemon wedges.

Serves 4

200 g (6 1/2 oz) scallops, roe removed
500 g (1 lb) cooked yabbies, peeled (and halved if large)
500 g (1 lb) cooked prawns (shrimp), peeled and deveined
250 g (8 oz) marinated mussels
2 tablespoons lime juice
1 tablespoon extra virgin olive oil
cracked black pepper
200 g (6 1/2 oz) orrechiette
150 g (5 oz) rocket (arugula)
lemon wedges, for serving

Dressing
1/4 cup whole egg mayonnaise
50 g (1 3/4 oz) plain yoghurt
1 tablespoon lime juice
50 g (1 3/4 oz) watercress leaves
2 teaspoons honey-cup mustard
1 tablespoon chopped fresh dill

We've taken the popular American crab cake and given it a lift. Use fresh crab if you can.

squiggly corn crab cakes

100 g (3 1/2 oz) corn spaghetti
500 g (1 lb) fresh or canned crab meat
1 small red capsicum (pepper), finely chopped
1 tablespoon capers, roughly chopped
2 tablespoons lime juice
1 teaspoon grated lime zest
1 teaspoon tabasco
6 spring (green) onions, chopped
1 egg, lightly beaten
1 1/2 cups fresh breadcrumbs
peanut (groundnut) oil, for shallow-frying
chilli jam, for serving

Cook the pasta in a large pan of rapidly boiling water until al dente. Drain well and lay out to dry on paper towels, then cut into short lengths.

Combine the pasta, crab, capsicum, capers, lime juice, zest, tabasco, spring onion, egg and breadcrumbs. Divide the mixture into eight and shape into patties. Place on a tray and refrigerate for 30 minutes.

Heat the oil in a large, deep frying pan to 180°C (350°F), or until a cube of bread browns in 15 seconds when dropped into the oil. Shallow-fry the crab cakes in batches for 3 minutes each side, or until crisp and golden brown. Serve with chilli jam.

Serves 4

Only the rind of preserved lemon
is used—discard the tender flesh
as it is much too bitter.

preserved lemon chicken with fettucine

Heat the oil in a large, deep frying pan, and cook the spices, onion and garlic over medium heat for 5 minutes, or until the onion is soft and the spices are fragrant.
Add the preserved lemon and chicken and cook over high heat until the chicken is browned. Add the lemon juice, stock, olives and butter and bring to the boil, then reduce the heat and simmer for 10 minutes. Remove from the heat and fold in the coriander.
Meanwhile, cook the pasta in a large pan of rapidly boiling water until al dente, then drain.
Toss the pasta through the sauce and serve immediately.

Serves 4

2 tablespoons oil
1 tablespoon ground cumin
1 tablespoon ground coriander
1/2 teaspoon cayenne pepper
1 onion, sliced
3 cloves garlic, sliced
1/2 preserved lemon, cut into fine shreds
400 g (13 oz) chicken thigh fillets, cut into thin strips
125 ml (4 fl oz) lemon juice
300 ml (10 fl oz) chicken stock
1 cup green olives stuffed with sun-dried tomatoes, sliced
50 g (13/4 oz) butter
1/2 cup fresh coriander (cilantro) leaves
400 g (13 oz) fettucine

If made in the north, this classic southern Italian soup would be thickened with rice not pasta.

hearty italian sausage minestrone

250 g (8 oz) dried borlotti beans, soaked overnight
2 tablespoons oil
2 cloves garlic, crushed
1 onion, chopped
2 celery sticks, diced
2 carrots, diced
2 potatoes, peeled and diced
2 tablespoons tomato paste
2 litres beef stock
1 bouquet garni
6 italian sausages with fennel (finnochio)
100 g (3 1/2 oz) ditalini
2 zucchini (courgettes), diced
1/4 cup chopped fresh parsley
parmesan shavings, for serving

Cook the beans in boiling water for 1 hour 30 minutes, or until tender. Meanwhile, heat the oil in a large heavy-based pan and cook the garlic and onion over medium heat until the onion is soft and golden. Add the celery, carrot and potato and cook, stirring, for 10 minutes, or until the vegetables are slightly browned. Stir in the tomato paste, stock and bouquet garni and bring to the boil, then reduce the heat and simmer for 40 minutes.

Grill or fry the sausages and then cut into bite-sized pieces. Drain the beans and add to the soup with the ditalini, zucchini and sausage. Simmer for 10 minutes, or until the pasta is soft. Season and stir in the parsley. Serve with the parmesan shavings.

Serves 6–8

Amazingly, the Italian Academy of
Cooking has set dimensions for
tagliatelle: 6 mm wide x 1 mm thick.

pumpkins with creamy bacon pasta

Preheat the oven to 180°C (350°F/
Gas 4). Cook the pasta in a large pan
of rapidly boiling water until al dente,
then drain. Cut into shorter pieces.
Meanwhile, heat the oil in a frying pan
and cook the leek and bacon over
medium heat for 5 minutes.
Add the wine, stir well and bring to the
boil. Stir in the cream and parmesan
and boil for 3 minutes, or until
thickened slightly. Add the pasta and
toss together.
Slice the tops off the pumpkins and
use a spoon to remove the seeds.
Fill the pumpkins with the pasta mixture,
then place on a baking tray with the
pumpkin tops. Bake for
40–50 minutes, or until the pumpkins
are tender. Replace the tops to serve.

Serves 4

100 g (3 1/2 oz) tagliatelle
1 tablespoon oil
1 leek, sliced
3 rashers bacon, chopped
125 ml (4 fl oz) white wine
250 ml (8 fl oz) cream
1/2 cup grated parmesan
4 large golden nugget pumpkins
(squash)

These slippery flat noodles take their name from the Italian word meaning 'little tongues'.

chilli linguine with scallops and lime

45 g (1¹/2 oz) butter
6 spring (green) onions, sliced
1 teaspoon grated fresh ginger
2 cloves garlic, crushed
1 fresh red chilli, finely chopped
500 g (1 lb) scallops
juice and rind of 1 lime
400 ml (13 fl oz) coconut cream
2 tablespoons fish sauce
1 tablespoon soft brown sugar
6 kaffir lime leaves, finely shredded,
plus a little extra for garnishing
250 g (8 oz) fresh chilli linguine

Melt 30 g (1 oz) of the butter in a large frying pan, add the spring onion, ginger, garlic and chilli and cook over medium heat for 2 minutes, or until the onion is golden. Remove from the pan. Reheat the pan to high, add the remaining butter and cook the scallops in batches over high heat until tender. Return the spring onion mixture to the pan and stir in the lime juice and rind, coconut cream, fish sauce, brown sugar and kaffir lime leaves. Simmer for 5 minutes, or until heated through. Meanwhile, cook the pasta in a large pan of boiling water until al dente, then drain well and twist into nests. Serve the sauce over the pasta and garnish with a few shredded kaffir lime leaves.

Serves 4

Gorgonzola is the town where cows were rested on the journey to the Alpine grazing slopes.

ruote with gorgonzola and peppered steak

Cook the pasta in a large pan of rapidly boiling water until al dente, then drain. Coat the rump steak in cracked black pepper. Heat the oil in a frying pan and cook the beef until medium rare. Allow to rest for 5 minutes before slicing. Add the steak, rocket, crumbled gorgonzola and pimentos to the pasta and toss together.
To make the dressing, place the red wine vinegar, honey, redcurrant jelly, oil and mustard in a pan and bring to the boil. Boil for 5 minutes, or until thickened slightly. Pour over the pasta and toss well. Serve immediately.

Serves 6

400 g (13 oz) ruote (pasta wheels)
500 g (1 lb) rump steak
cracked black pepper
1 tablespoon oil
1 bunch rocket (arugula)
250 g (8 oz) gorgonzola
300 g (10 oz) bottled pimentos, drained and sliced

Dressing
100 ml (3$1/2$ fl oz) red wine vinegar
2 tablespoons honey
2 tablespoons redcurrant jelly
50 ml (1$3/4$ fl oz) extra virgin olive oil
1 tablespoon seeded mustard

Gnocchi are little Italian dumplings, traditionally made from semolina flour or potato.

gnocchi three-cheese bake

500 g (1 lb) fresh gnocchi
150 g (5 oz) blue cheese
300 ml (10 fl oz) cream
50 g (1³/4 oz) fontina cheese, thinly sliced
50 g (1³/4 oz) provolone cheese, thinly sliced

Cook the gnocchi in a large pan of boiling water for about 2 minutes, or until they float to the surface. Remove and drain well, then spoon into 6 individual ovenproof dishes.

Heat the blue cheese and cream in a frying pan over low heat until combined, then bring to the boil and cook until the sauce thickens enough to coat the back of a spoon.

Pour the blue cheese sauce over the gnocchi, then lay the cheese slices over the top. Cook under a preheated grill until golden brown.

Serves 6 as a first course

Barbecued ducks are available in chinatowns the world over. Ask to have the bones removed.

orange poppy seed pappardelle with duck

Preheat the oven to 220°C (425°F/ Gas 7). Place the vegetables in a baking dish, drizzle with olive oil and sprinkle with sea salt and cracked black pepper. Roast for 30 minutes, then add the garlic and roast for 10 minutes. Meanwhile, cook the pasta in a large pan of rapidly boiling water until al dente, then drain.
Combine the poppy seeds, orange juice, mustard, vinegar, sesame oil and five spice to make a dressing. Toss two thirds of the dressing through the pasta.
Top the pasta with the roasted vegetables and the duck. Sprinkle with the chives and drizzle with the remaining dressing.

Serves 4–6

3 parsnips, quartered
1 bunch baby carrots
300 g (10 oz) sweet potatoes, peeled and cut into large chunks
200 g (6 1/2 oz) kipfler potatoes, unpeeled and quartered
3 tablespoons olive oil
10 unpeeled cloves garlic
300 g (10 oz) pappardelle
2 tablespoons poppy seeds
180 ml (6 fl oz) orange juice
1 tablespoon dijon mustard
3 tablespoons tarragon vinegar
2 teaspoons sesame oil
1/2 teaspoon five spice
1 chinese barbecued duck, bones removed, cut into pieces
2 tablespoons snipped fresh garlic chives

Fettucine is often confused with tagliatelle, but is actually slightly narrower and thicker.

vegetable pasta torte

4 small roma tomatoes
300 g (10 oz) sweet potatoes, peeled and cut into large chunks
1 red capsicum (pepper)
3 tablespoons oil
200 g (6¹/2 oz) fettucine
6 eggs, lightly beaten
250 ml (8 fl oz) milk
1 cup grated cheddar cheese
¹/2 cup flat-leaf parsley
200 g (6¹/2 oz) feta cheese, cut into large cubes

Preheat the oven to 200°C (400°F/ Gas 6). Place the tomatoes, sweet potato and capsicum in a baking dish, drizzle with oil and season well. Bake for 40 minutes, or until tender. Peel the capsicum and cut into large chunks. Cook the pasta in rapidly boiling water until al dente, then drain well. Combine the egg, milk and cheddar. Arrange half the vegetables and half the parsley in a greased 24 cm (10 inch) non-stick deep frying pan. Top with half the pasta and feta, then layer with the remaining vegetables, parsley, pasta and feta. Top with the egg mix. Cook over medium heat for 15–20 minutes, or until just set (be careful not to burn the base). Grill for 15–20 minutes, or until the top is golden brown. Leave for 5 minutes before turning out to serve.

Serves 6–8

This is a really quick and simple
'cheat's ravioli', using wonton
wrappers instead of pasta.

chicken ravioli with coriander

Mix together the chicken mince, sweet
chilli sauce, coriander, sesame oil and
lime rind. Place a heaped tablespoon of
the mixture in the centre of a wonton
wrapper, lightly brush the edges with
water and top with another wrapper.
Press the edges together to seal.
Repeat with the remaining chicken filling
and wrappers.
Cook the ravioli in batches in a large
pan of rapidly boiling water
for 5 minutes, then drain well and place
on serving plates.
Meanwhile, combine the fish sauce,
sugar, peanut oil and lime juice. Pour
over the ravioli and garnish with the red
chilli and extra coriander leaves.

Serves 4 as a first course

400 g (13 oz) chicken mince (ground
  chicken)
2 tablespoons sweet chilli sauce
3 tablespoons chopped fresh
  coriander (cilantro), plus extra
  leaves for garnishing
1 1/2 teaspoons sesame oil
2 teaspoons grated lime rind
200 g (6 1/2 oz) wonton wrappers
125 ml (4 fl oz) fish sauce
2 tablespoons soft brown sugar
1 tablespoon peanut (groundnut) oil
1 tablespoon lime juice
1 fresh red chilli, finely sliced

Dishes from the region around
Nice typically feature olives,
tomatoes, beans and anchovies.

salmon nicoise with little pasta ears

250 g (8 oz) orrechiette
500 g (1 lb) salmon fillet
2 tablespoons oil
200 g (6¹/2 oz) green beans
1 cup marinated kalamata olives
1 red capsicum (pepper), chopped
100 g (3¹/2 oz) cherry tomatoes,
halved
1 red onion, cut into very fine slivers
6 anchovies, halved lengthways
100 g (3¹/2 oz) baby english
spinach leaves
4 hard-boiled eggs, quartered

Dressing
3 tablespoons olive oil
3 tablespoons lemon juice
1 tablespoon wholegrain mustard
2 tablespoons chopped fresh dill
1 teaspoon honey

Cook the pasta in a large pan of rapidly boiling water until al dente, then drain. Remove the skin and any bones from the salmon and cut into large chunks. Heat the oil in a pan and cook the salmon in batches over high heat until crisp and browned—take care not to overcook or it will fall apart in the salad. Cook the beans in boiling water until tender, then drain. Gently toss together the salmon, beans, olives, capsicum, cherry tomatoes, onion, anchovies and pasta.

Serve on a bed of baby spinach leaves. Top with the eggs. Whisk together the dressing ingredients and pour over the salad.

Serves 6

Anyone who enjoys smoked fish chowder or fish pie will go weak at the knees for this dish.

smoked cod pasta and potato mornay

Preheat the oven to 200°C (400°F/ Gas 6). Boil the potato until tender, then mash until smooth with 60 g (2 oz) of the butter, the garlic and 125 ml (4 fl oz) of the milk. Cook the pasta in rapidly boiling water until al dente. Drain and spoon into a 2.5 litre ovenproof dish. Heat the oil and remaining butter in a large frying pan and cook the leek and fennel for 5 minutes, or until soft. Add the capers and flour and cook, stirring, for 1 minute. Remove from the heat and gradually stir in the cream and remaining milk. Return to the heat and stir until the sauce boils and thickens. Add the dill, half the parmesan and the cod and pour over the pasta. Top with the mash and the remaining cheese. Bake for 20 minutes, or until golden brown. Serve with lemon wedges.

Serves 4

4 potatoes, peeled and chopped
90 g (3 oz) butter
1 clove garlic, crushed
625 ml (20 fl oz) milk
200 g (6 1/2 oz) fusilli
1 tablespoon oil
1 leek, thinly sliced
4 baby fennel, thinly sliced
2 tablespoons capers, roughly chopped
1–2 tablespoons plain (all-purpose) flour
125 ml (4 fl oz) cream
3 tablespoons chopped fresh dill
1/2 cup grated parmesan
300 g (10 oz) smoked cod, chopped
lemon wedges, for serving

Chorizo is a spicy Spanish
sausage of smoked pork,
flavoured with garlic and paprika.

rigatoni with chorizo, chipotle and deep-fried basil

1 tablespoon oil
1 red onion, sliced
4 chorizo sausages, cut into thick
slices on an angle
400 g (13 oz) can chopped tomatoes
2 canned chipotle chillies, chopped
oil, for shallow-frying
fresh basil leaves
500 g (1 lb) rigatoni

Heat the oil in a large frying pan and cook the onion over medium heat for 3 minutes, or until soft. Add the sausage and cook for 5 minutes, draining off any excess oil. Add the tomato and chipotle chillies and bring to the boil. Reduce the heat and simmer for 15 minutes, or until the sauce has thickened slightly.

Heat 4 cm (2 inches) oil in a deep frying pan over medium heat and shallow-fry the basil in batches until crisp. Drain on paper towels.

Meanwhile, cook the pasta in a large pan of rapidly boiling water until al dente, then drain.

Serve the sauce over the pasta and garnish with the deep-fried basil.

Serves 4

Pesto literally means 'pounded' and the sauce is traditionally prepared in a mortar and pestle.

spaghetti pesto

Cook the pasta in a large pan of rapidly boiling water until al dente, then drain. Place the basil, salt, garlic, pine nuts and parmesan in a food processor and process until the mixture forms a smooth paste (take care not to overprocess or you will bruise the basil). With the motor running, gradually add the olive oil in a thin stream until it is well combined. Add the pesto to the spaghetti and toss together. Serve immediately with the parmesan.

Serves 4

400 g (13 oz) spaghetti
2 cups fresh basil
pinch of salt
2 cloves garlic
1/4 cup pine nuts, toasted
1/2 cup grated parmesan
80 ml (2 3/4 fl oz) extra virgin olive oil
shaved parmesan, for serving

These little pasta frittatas
are ideal for serving hot or
cold as a brunch dish.

smoked chicken, brie and cranberry pasta nests

200 g (6¹/2 oz) fresh spinach or herb
tagliatelle
2 smoked chicken breasts, sliced
200 g (6¹/2 oz) double cream brie,
sliced
2 tablespoons snipped fresh chives
8 eggs, lightly beaten
125 ml (4 fl oz) cream
¹/2 cup grated smoked cheddar
cheese
2 tablespoons cranberry sauce

Preheat the oven to 180°C (350°F/
Gas 4). Cook the pasta in a large pan
of rapidly boiling water until al dente,
then drain and pat dry.
Lightly grease six 250 ml (8 fl oz) muffin
holes and line the bases and sides with
the pasta.
Arrange the smoked chicken slices
around the inside of the pasta and fill
the centre with the brie. Sprinkle with
the chives.
Whisk together the egg, cream and
cheese and pour into the nests. Top
each one with a teaspoonful of the
cranberry sauce and swirl gently with a
skewer. Bake for 20 minutes,
or until set.

Makes 6

You could use twelve 125 ml (4 fl oz)
muffin holes to make miniature nests.

If you aren't a lover of goats cheese, feta and ricotta both work well in this dish.

smoked trout, eggplant and goats cheese stacks

Lightly brush the eggplant with olive oil and grill until golden brown on both sides.

Cut the lasagne sheets into twelve 8 cm (3 inch) squares. Cook in batches in a large pan of rapidly boiling water until al dente. Drain well.

Place one sheet of lasagne on the centre of each plate. Top with a folded slice of smoked trout, a slice of eggplant and a slice of goats cheese. Top with another sheet of lasagne and layer as before. Finish with a curl of smoked trout, crumbled goats cheese and a sprinkling of semi-dried tomato.

To make the sauce, heat the butter, parsley, stock, lime juice and pepper in a pan. Drizzle over the stacks and serve immediately.

Serves 4

1 medium eggplant (aubergine) cut into 8 thick slices
olive oil
375 g (12 oz) fresh lasagne sheets
200 g (6¹/2 oz) smoked trout or salmon
200 g (6¹/2 oz) goats cheese, cut into thick slices
150 g (5 oz) semi-dried tomatoes, chopped

Sauce
50 g (1³/4 oz) butter
2 tablespoons roughly chopped fresh parsley
250 ml (8 fl oz) chicken stock
3 tablespoons lime juice
cracked black pepper

Balsamic vinegar, from Modena, is
aged in oak barrels for up to 15 years.
Like good wine, it improves with age.

warm casarecci salad

750 g (1 1/2 lb) orange sweet potato
2 tablespoons extra virgin olive oil
500 g (1 lb) casarecci
325 g (11 oz) marinated feta in oil
3 tablespoons balsamic vinegar
1 bunch asparagus, cut into
short lengths
100 g (3 1/2 oz) baby rocket or baby
english spinach leaves
2 vine-ripened tomatoes, chopped
1/4 cup pine nuts, toasted

Preheat the oven to 200°C (400°F).
Peel the sweet potato and cut into
large pieces. Place in a baking dish,
drizzle with the olive oil and season
generously with sea salt and cracked
black pepper. Bake for 20 minutes, or
until the sweet potato is tender.
Cook the pasta in a large pan of rapidly
boiling water until al dente. Drain well.
Drain the oil from the feta and whisk
three tablespoons of the oil with the
balsamic vinegar to make a dressing.
Steam or microwave the asparagus
until bright green and tender. Drain well.
Combine the pasta, sweet potato,
asparagus, rocket, feta, tomatoes and
pine nuts in a bowl. Add the dressing
and toss gently. Season with black
pepper and serve immediately.

Serves 4

'Alla puttanesca' signifies a tomato-based sauce, containing olives, anchovies and capers.

penne puttanesca

Heat the oil in a pan and cook the onion, garlic and chillies over medium heat for 5 minutes, or until the onion is tender.

Add the tomato, white wine and bay leaf and bring to the boil. Reduce the heat and simmer for 15 minutes. Season with the balsamic vinegar, sugar and salt and pepper to taste.

Add the anchovy, capers and olives and simmer for 5 minutes, or until heated through.

Meanwhile, cook the pasta in a large pan of rapidly boiling water until al dente. Drain well.

Remove the bay leaf from the sauce and stir in the parsley. Toss with the pasta and serve with grated parmesan.

Serves 4–6

2 tablespoons oil
1 onion, finely chopped
3 cloves garlic, crushed
2 red chillies, finely chopped
800 g (1 lb 10 oz) canned chopped tomatoes
125 ml (4 fl oz) dry white wine
1 bay leaf
1 tablespoon balsamic vinegar
1 teaspoon sugar
6 anchovy fillets, chopped
2 tablespoons capers, chopped
200 g (6 1/2 oz) marinated black olives, pitted and chopped
500 g (1 lb) penne rigate
2 tablespoons chopped fresh parsley
grated parmesan, for serving

A new twist on an old favourite—
beef stroganoff—this is a quick
and easy creamy pasta meal.

lamb pasta stroganoff

400 g (13 oz) fresh herb spaghetti
2 tablespoons oil
450 g (14 oz) lamb fillet
50 g (1 3/4 oz) butter
1 onion, sliced
200 g (6 1/2 oz) button mushrooms,
sliced
2 tablespoons tomato paste
1 tablespoon wholegrain mustard
300 g (10 oz) sour cream
1 tablespoon fresh thyme leaves

Cook the pasta in a large pan of rapidly boiling water until al dente. Drain well. Heat the oil in a large frying pan and cook the lamb over high heat until browned and medium rare. Leave to stand for 5 minutes before slicing thinly. Melt the butter in the pan and cook the onion over medium heat for 3 minutes, or until golden. Add the mushrooms and cook until browned. Remove the onion and mushrooms and set aside. Return the lamb to the pan and add the tomato paste and mustard. Lower the heat, add the sour cream and cook until heated through (do not allow to boil or the sour cream will split). Toss the sauce through the pasta. Serve topped with the onion and mushrooms and sprinkled with thyme.

Serves 4

Saffron, which comes from the dried stigma of the crocus flower, is a spice more costly than gold.

saffron fettucine with garlic seafood

Cook the pasta in a large pan of rapidly boiling water until al dente, then drain. Heat the oil and cook the seafood in batches until the scallops and fish turn white and the prawns pink. Remove from the pan and keep warm. Add the wine to the pan and bring to the boil, stirring well to mix in any bits that are stuck to the bottom of the pan. Add the butter, garlic and spring onion and cook over medium heat until soft. Return the seafood to the pan to gently reheat and add the zest and chives. Twist the pasta into nests and serve topped with the seafood.

Serves 4

375 g (12 oz) fresh saffron fettucine
1 tablespoon extra virgin olive oil
200 g (6 1/2 oz) scallops
500 g (1 lb) raw prawns (shrimp), peeled and deveined, with the tails left intact
200 g (6 1/2 oz) firm white fish fillets, cut into large pieces
125 ml (4 fl oz) dry white wine
100 g (3 1/2 oz) butter
3 cloves garlic, crushed
4 spring (green) onions, sliced
zest of 1 lime
1 tablespoon snipped fresh chives

The Italian woodcutter (boscaiola)
would collect the mushrooms for
this sauce during his day's work.

ziti with brandy boscaiola

500 g (1 lb) ziti
80 g (2³/4 oz) butter
6 rashers bacon, sliced
6 french shallots, sliced
2 tablespoons brandy
750 g (1¹/2 lb) mixed wild
mushrooms
2 teaspoons fresh thyme
250 ml (8 fl oz) chicken stock
250 ml (8 fl oz) cream

Cook the pasta in a large pan of rapidly
boiling water until al dente, then drain.
Melt half the butter in a large frying pan
and cook the bacon and shallots over
high heat until crisp and browned. Stir
in the brandy and bring to the boil,
stirring to incorporate any bits stuck to
the bottom of the pan.
Add the remaining butter to the pan,
add the mushrooms and cook to
soften. Stir in the thyme, stock and
cream and bring to the boil. Reduce
the heat and simmer for 5 minutes, or
until the sauce has thickened slightly.
Serve on top of or tossed through
the pasta.

Serves 4

Also known as riso orzo, risoni is
a rice-shaped pasta that is often
added to soups to thicken them.

artichoke risoni

Heat the butter and olive oil in a frying
pan and cook the fennel over medium
heat for 20 minutes, or until
caramelized. Add the artichoke and
cook for 5–10 minutes longer.
Add the cream, mustard, wine and
parmesan and bring to the boil.
Reduce the heat and simmer for
5 minutes.
Meanwhile, cook the pasta in a large
pan of rapidly boiling water
until al dente, then drain well.
Add the risoni and spinach to the
sauce and cook until the spinach has
wilted. Excellent served on toasted
Italian bread.

Serves 4

30 g (1 oz) butter
1 tablespoon olive oil
2 fennel bulbs, sliced
340 g (11 oz) marinated artichoke
    hearts, drained and chopped
300 ml (10 fl oz) cream
1 tablespoon dijon mustard
3 tablespoons dry white wine
1/2 cup grated parmesan
375 g (12 oz) risoni
2 cups shredded english spinach

We've roasted our ratatouille,
rather than simmering, so the
vegetables keep their chunkiness.

roasted chunky ratatouille cannelloni

1 medium eggplant (aubergine)
2 zucchini (courgettes)
1 large red capsicum (pepper)
1 large green capsicum (pepper)
3–4 ripe roma tomatoes
12 unpeeled cloves garlic
3 tablespoons olive oil
300 ml (10 fl oz) italian tomato passata
350 g (12 oz) cannelloni tubes
3 tablespoons shredded fresh basil
300 g (10 oz) ricotta cheese
100 g (3 1/2 oz) feta cheese
1 egg, lightly beaten
50 g (1 3/4 oz) pecorino pepato cheese, grated

Preheat the oven to 200°C (400°F/ Gas 6). Cut the eggplant, zucchini, capsicums and tomatoes into 2 cm (1 inch) cubes and place in a baking dish with the garlic. Drizzle with the olive oil and toss to coat. Bake for 1 hour 30 minutes, or until the vegetables are tender and the tomatoes slightly mushy. Peel the garlic and lightly mash.

Pour the passata over the base of a large ovenproof dish. Spoon the ratatouille into the cannelloni tubes and arrange in the dish.

Combine the basil, ricotta, feta and egg, season well and spoon over the cannelloni. Sprinkle with the pecorino and bake for 30 minutes, or until the cannelloni is soft.

Serves 6–8

The name carbonara ('charcoal-style') is a mystery... perhaps it is the coalminers' favourite dish?

farfalle with parma ham carbonara

Cook the pasta in a large pan of rapidly boiling water until al dente. Drain and return to the pan. Cook the parma ham in a non-stick pan until crisp. Whisk together the eggs, parmesan and cream, then stir in the ham.
Pour the sauce over the warm pasta in the pan and toss gently to coat. Return to the heat and cook gently for 1 minute, or until slightly thickened. Be careful not to overheat or the eggs will begin to scramble.

Serves 4

500 g (1 lb) farfalle
10 thin slices parma ham or bacon, chopped
4 eggs
1 cup grated parmesan
250 ml (8 fl oz) cream

Concha is the Latin word for
'shell' and these elegant shapes
are perfect for holding fillings.

conchiglie stuffed with roast pumpkin and ricotta

1 kg (2 lb) butternut pumpkin (squash),
cut into large wedges
olive oil
10 unpeeled cloves garlic
500 g (1 lb) ricotta cheese
1/3 cup finely shredded fresh basil
750 ml (24 fl oz) bottled italian pasta
sauce (pomodoro)
125 ml (4 fl oz) dry white wine
56 conchiglie (or 32 giant conchiglie)
1 cup grated parmesan

Preheat the oven to 200°C (400°F/
Gas 6). Place the pumpkin in a baking
dish, drizzle with olive oil and season.
Bake for 30 minutes, add the garlic and
bake for 20 minutes, or until tender.
Cool slightly, then peel and mash the
pumpkin and garlic. Mix with the ricotta
and half the basil and season to taste.
Put the pasta sauce and wine in a pan
and bring to the boil, then simmer for
10 minutes, or until slightly thickened.
Cook the pasta in rapidly boiling water
until al dente. Lay out on a tea towel to
dry, then fill with the pumpkin mix.
Spread any remaining filling in a large
ovenproof dish, top with the shells,
pour over the sauce and sprinkle with
the parmesan and remaining basil.
Bake for 15–20 minutes (or 30 minutes
for the giant shells).

Serves 6

These simple pasta pots serve well as a delicious first course for a dinner party.

rigatoni, asparagus and saffron chicken pots

Cook the pasta in a large pan of rapidly boiling water until al dente, then drain. Heat the oil and half the butter in a large frying pan and brown the chicken in batches over high heat until cooked through. Remove and keep warm. Add the remaining butter, garlic, spring onion and asparagus to the pan and cook, stirring, until the asparagus is bright green. Add the tomato and cook until all the liquid has been absorbed. Stir in the saffron and wine and bring to the boil. Reduce the heat, sprinkle with the flour and gradually add the milk. Cook, stirring, until the mixture boils and thickens. Stir in the parmesan. Add the chicken and any juices to the pan and heat through. Stir in the pasta. Divide among 4 gratin or soufflé dishes and grill until golden brown.

Serves 4 as a first course

300 g (10 oz) rigatoni
1 tablespoon oil
60 g (2 oz) butter
4 chicken thigh fillets, cut into thin strips
2 cloves garlic, crushed
4 spring (green) onions, sliced
1 bunch asparagus, cut into short lengths
3 ripe tomatoes, peeled, seeded and chopped
1/4 teaspoon saffron threads
3 tablespoons white wine
2 tablespoons plain (all-purpose) flour
315 ml (10 fl oz) milk
1 cup grated parmesan

Baby bocconcini are tiny balls of
fresh mozzarella. Store them in
the whey you buy them in.

fusilli with roasted tomatoes, tapenade and bocconcini

800 g (1 lb 10 oz) cherry or teardrop
tomatoes (or a mixture of both),
halved if they are large
500 g (1 lb) fusilli
300 g (10 oz) baby bocconcini, sliced
1 tablespoon fresh thyme

Tapenade
1 1/2 tablespoons capers
45 g (1 1/2 oz) drained anchovy fillets
75 g (2 1/2 oz) tuna in oil, drained
2 small cloves garlic
1 1/2 cups sliced black olives
3 tablespoons fresh lemon juice
4–5 tablespoons extra virgin olive oil

Preheat the oven to 200°C (400°F/
Gas 6). Place the tomatoes on a
baking tray, sprinkle with salt and
pepper and bake for 10 minutes, or
until slightly dried.

To make the tapenade, place the
capers, anchovies, tuna, garlic, olives
and lemon juice in a food processor
and mix together. With the motor
running, gradually add the oil until the
mixture forms a smooth paste.

Cook the pasta in a large pan of rapidly
boiling water until al dente, then drain.
Toss the tapenade and bocconcini
through the hot pasta.

Top with the roasted tomatoes and
thyme and serve immediately.

Serves 4–6

Primavera is Italian for 'spring' and this dish traditionally features vibrant young spring vegetables.

crunchy primavera spaghetti

Cook the pasta in a large pan of rapidly boiling water until al dente, then drain. Meanwhile, cook the vegetables separately in boiling water until tender and drain well.
Heat the butter and oil in a large frying pan, add the garlic and breadcrumbs and cook over medium heat until the breadcrumbs are crisp and golden. Toss through the parmesan. Add to the pasta with the cream and toss together. Add the vegetables, quickly toss and serve drizzled with balsamic vinegar and sprinkled with parmesan shavings.

Serves 4–6

400 g (13 oz) spaghetti
1 cup broad (fava) beans, fresh or frozen
300 g (10 oz) sugar snap peas
2 bunches asparagus, cut into short lengths
60 g (2 oz) butter
2 tablespoons extra virgin olive oil
2 cloves garlic, crushed
3 cups fresh white breadcrumbs
1/4 cup finely grated parmesan
3 tablespoons cream
2 tablespoons balsamic vinegar
shaved parmesan, for serving

Chermoula is a Moroccan
marinade often used with fish.
Most families have their own recipe.

chilli linguine with chermoula chicken

600 g (1 1/4 lb) chicken breast fillets
500 g (1 lb) chilli linguine

Chermoula
2 cups fresh coriander (cilantro)
leaves, chopped
2 cups fresh flat-leaf parsley leaves,
chopped
4 cloves garlic, crushed
2 teaspoons ground cumin
2 teaspoons ground paprika
125 ml (4 fl oz) lemon juice
2 teaspoons lemon rind
100 ml (3 1/2 fl oz) olive oil

Cook the chicken breasts in a non-
stick frying pan until tender. Leave for
5 minutes before cutting into thin slices.
Cook the pasta in a large pan of rapidly
boiling water until al dente, then drain.
Meanwhile, combine the chermoula
ingredients in a glass bowl and add the
sliced chicken. Leave to stand until the
pasta has finished cooking.
Serve the pasta topped with the
chermoula chicken.

Serves 4

lasagne

Heat the oil in a large pan and cook the garlic, onion, pancetta, carrot, celery and mushrooms for 5 minutes, stirring. Increase the heat, add the beef and brown well, breaking up any lumps. Add the tomato, wine, stock, oregano, bay leaf and tomato paste. Bring to the boil, stirring, then simmer for 50 minutes. Steam the spinach to wilt; squeeze dry.

To make the cheese sauce, melt the butter in a heavy-based pan and cook the flour for 1 minute to make a smooth paste. Remove from the heat and slowly stir in the milk until smooth. Return to the heat and stir until the sauce boils and thickens. Cook over low heat for a minute, then stir in the ricotta, nutmeg and parmesan and cook until melted.

Preheat the oven to 180°C (350°F/ Gas 4). Grease a 34 x 22 x 7 cm (14 x 9 x 3 inch) ovenproof dish. Layer a third of the meat sauce, then lasagne sheets, then 3/4 cup of cheese sauce. Top with half the spinach and half the fontina. Continue layering and top with the parmesan. Bake for 45 minutes.

Serves 6–8

1 tablespoon olive oil
2 cloves garlic, crushed
1 large onion, chopped
50 g (13/4 oz) pancetta, chopped
1 large carrot, grated
1 celery stick, chopped
125 g (4 oz) mushrooms, chopped
1 kg (2 lb) minced (ground) beef
600 g (11/4 lb) can chopped tomatoes
250 ml (8 fl oz) red wine
250 ml (8 fl oz) beef stock
1 teaspoon dried oregano
1 bay leaf
3 tablespoons tomato paste
500 g (1 lb) english spinach
250 g (8 oz) fresh lasagne sheets
250 g (8 oz) fontina cheese, thinly sliced
100 g (31/2 oz) parmesan, grated

Cheese sauce
60 g (2 oz) butter
1/3 cup plain (all-purpose) flour
500 ml (16 fl oz) milk
200 g (61/2 oz) ricotta cheese
1/2 teaspoon ground nutmeg
50 g (13/4 oz) parmesan, grated

Wrongly thought to be a
vegetable, the eggplant is actually
a berry... a very large one at that!

spicy eggplant spaghetti

300 g (10 oz) spaghetti
125 ml (4 fl oz) extra virgin olive oil
2 fresh red chillies, finely sliced
1 onion, finely chopped
3 cloves garlic, crushed
4 rashers bacon, chopped
400 g (13 oz) eggplant (aubergine),
diced
2 tablespoons balsamic vinegar
2 tomatoes, chopped
3 tablespoons shredded fresh basil
50 g (1³/4 oz) pecorino pepato
cheese, grated

Cook the pasta in a large pan of rapidly
boiling water until al dente, then drain.
Heat 1 tablespoon of the oil in a large,
deep frying pan and cook the chilli,
onion, garlic and bacon over medium
heat for 5 minutes, or until the onion is
golden and the bacon browned.
Remove from the pan and set aside.
Add half the remaining oil to the pan
and cook half the eggplant over high
heat, tossing to brown on all sides.
Remove and repeat with the remaining
oil and eggplant. Return the bacon
mixture and all the eggplant to the pan,
add the vinegar, tomato and
2 tablespoons basil and cook until
heated through. Season well.
Serve the spaghetti topped with the
eggplant and sprinkled with the grated
cheese and remaining basil.

Serves 4 as a first course

Published by Murdoch Books®, a division of Murdoch Magazines Pty Ltd,
45 Jones Street, Ultimo NSW 2007

Recipes: Jody Vassallo
Photography: Ben Dearnley
Stylist: Kristen Anderson
Food Stylist's Assistant: Michaela Le Compte
Concept and Design: Marylouise Brammer
Project Manager: Anna Waddington
Editor: Jane Price
Recipe Testing: Michaela Le Compte

CEO & Publisher: Anne Wilson
Associate Publisher: Catie Ziller
General Manager: Mark Smith
International Sales Director: Mark Newman
Marketing Manager: Beth Drumm
National Sales Manager (News Trade): Claire Connolly
Key Accounts Manager: Luke Elworthy

National Library of Australia Cataloguing-in-Publication Data
Vassallo, Jody.
Pasta.
Includes index.
ISBN 0 86411 900 3.
1. Cookery (Pasta). I. Title II. Title: Marie Claire (North Sydney, NSW).
641.822

Printed by Paramount. First printed 1999.
PRINTED IN HONG KONG.